*The
Magic
of
Words*

Con Felicidades
y
Nuestros Mejores Deseos
para
Un Feliz y Próspero
Año Nuevo

1983

Blackwell North America, Inc.
Lake Oswego, Oregon
y
Blackwood, New Jersey

The
Magic of Words

Rudolfo A. Anaya
and His Writings

Edited by
Paul Vassallo

University of New Mexico Press: *Albuquerque*

Library of Congress Cataloging in Publication Data
Main entry under title:

The Magic of words.

  Contents: Rudolfo Anaya/Frank Waters—In
commemoration: one million volumes/Rudolfo A.
Anaya—En conmemoración: un millón de volúmenes/
[R. A. Anaya; translated by] Matilde J. Farren—[etc.]
  1. Anaya, Rudolfo A.—Criticism and interpretation—
Addresses, essays, lectures. II. Vassallo, Paul.
PS3551.N27Z77 1982   813'.54   82-16024
ISBN 0-8263-0634-9

Rudolfo A. Anaya, "In Commemoration: One Million Volumes"
originally appeared in A MILLON STARS: THE MILLIONTH ACQUISI-
TION FOR THE UNIVERSITY OF NEW MEXICO GENERAL LIBRARY,
edited by Connie Capers Thorson (Albuquerque: The University of
New Mexico General Library, 1981) and is reproduced with per-
mission.

Contents

Preface

PAUL VASSALLO

NEW MEXICANS, WHETHER they be Native Americans from Ácoma or the Navajo Nation, descendants of the conquistadores from Tierra Amarilla, oil rig workers who followed the explorations from Texas, or recent newcomers like me, are proud of New Mexico—its history, heritage, diversity, and life. New Mexicans are also proud of the contributions the state has made and continues to make in the sciences, literature, and the arts. Thus, in 1981 when the time came for the celebration of the University of New Mexico General Library reaching its one millionth acquisition, a committee composed of individuals extending beyond the university and including a prominent lawyer, a leading restaurateur, an oil man, a well-known southwest author, the governor's wife, and others, decided that this was to be a celebration marked by excellence. That spirit of a pride in excellence was evident not only in the selection of the rare volumes comprising the millionth acquisition and a ceremony marked with joy and exuberance, but also in the selection of an author to write an essay to be included in a commemorative volume.

A native New Mexican, an accomplished author, a lover of culture and books, a university professor, *un hombre muy simpático*—when you combine these attributes with a man of feeling (it is much better in Spanish: *un hombre con ánima*)—then in New Mexico, you can only think of Rudolfo A. Anaya. Others in this book write more eloquently than I can of Rudy's stature, of his contributions to the literature of the southwest. Suffice it to say that we were proud to have his essay, "In Commemoration: One Million Volumes," included in the commemorative volume *A Million Stars*. We were also proud to have Rudy read portions of his essay as part of the proceedings at the ceremony celebrating the event.

Those attending the ceremony, those reading the commemorative volume, those from New Mexico, those who joined in the celebration from other parts of the country and Mexico, all were touched by Rudy's essay of joy in his discovery of the world of books. Innumerable requests to reprint the essay came in, and discussions to determine the best way of doing this started immediately. We all felt that this should be a project of the University of New Mexico General Library and a publication of the University of New Mexico Press.

At this same time, Blackwell North America, Inc., a leading international book distribution agency, started a project sponsoring special print runs by selected American small presses, giving wider recognition to those productions through distribution of copies as gifts to librarians and libraries, primarily in the United States. Jack Walsdorf brought the Anaya essay to the attention of his colleagues at Blackwell's, and their interest served as a stimulus for the project resulting in this publication.

New Mexico is proud of its Hispanic heritage. This heritage is reflected in Rudy Anaya's works, and a Spanish translation of his essay, done by Matilde J. Farren, is included in this volume.

The General Library is fortunate to be the repository of Rudy Anaya's literary papers. Teresa Márquez, reference librarian, played a key role in this acquisition. She is making another contribution in the form of a definitive annotated bibliography of works by and about Rudolfo Anaya.

Antonio Márquez, Assistant Professor of English at the University of New Mexico and a specialist in southwestern literature and contemporary and comparative literature, has contributed a critical analysis of Rudolfo Anaya's work to this volume.

Donald Farren, Head of the Special Collections Department in the General Library, selected the illustrations and has written a brief description. Those came from a collection of woodblocks included in the Laughing Horse Press archives.

Frank Waters, whose love of life, history, culture, and the people of the southwest is so vividly portrayed in his many literary contributions, is one of the most noted and honored figures in southwestern literature. His sensitivity to his surroundings and those he touches is evident in his writings. It is also evident in the *"Appreciative Footnote"* Frank Waters has contributed to this volume.

This has been a labor of love. The contributors have a respect and love for Rudy. The project evolved, almost as a family affair, with enthusiasm and dedication.

The
Magic
of
Words

*The
Magic
of
Words*

Rudolfo A. Anaya
An Appreciative Footnote

FRANK WATERS

RUDOLFO ANAYA'S ESSAY, reprinted here from the volume commemorating the University of New Mexico General Library's acquisition of its millionth volume, recounts his introduction to the world of books in the dusty one-room library of a hundred books in his small village of Santa Rosa. We follow his boyhood enchantment with the magic of the printed word through the Albuquerque High School library and the University's great library of a million volumes, to his present work as a mature professor and a novelist of distinction writing books of his own. A million volumes, an immeasurable world of books! A magic realm of learning, imagination, and power.

Anaya describes this as a rite of passage from innocence are swallowed by this sea of proliferating print, becoming into knowledge of the world. Unfortunately, many of us academic bookworms who footnote all our opinions with references to some volume, page, and paragraph. Attired in gowns and caps, we often forget that there exists a knowledge imprinted on no page, but recorded during childhood in our hearts and minds.

Rudolfo Anaya's writing achieves a reconciliation of this dichotomy between natural feeling and acquired intellectual knowledge. Perhaps these dual influences were symbolized in his native homeland by the *llanos,* the wide free plains of the *vaqueros,* and the *barrios* of the settled farmers.

Anaya never forgets his childhood. Almost everything he has written casts back to his earliest years in Santa Rosa, and bears the stamp of his Spanish-Indian heritage. Now known as Chicano, it has its own unique traditions, folklore, images, and oral folktales. Members of the still-developing Chicano social movement are spread over most of the Southwest, being most predominant in New Mexico and southern Colorado. United by pride in their mixed ancestry, they are developing Chicano literature within the general field of Anglo-American, Mexican-American, and Spanish-American literature.

There is little need to record here Anaya's emergence from this field as one of the foremost Chicano writers. The phenomenal success of his first novel *Bless Me, Ultima* (1972) was followed by *Heart of Aztlán* (1976) and *Tortuga* (1979). All were issued by Chicano publishers, further establishing his reputation.

A critical analysis of his work is given in this volume by Antonio Márquez, more competent than I to assume such a task. I can venture here only a personal observation. It seems to me that what may account for the wide popularity

4

of Anaya's novels is not their background, significant and unusual as it is, but the childish innocence and freshness they all contain. *Bless Me, Ultima,* in fact, is written in first person from the viewpoint of a ten-year-old boy. So is the heartrending *Tortuga. Heart of Aztlán,* embracing a wider and social field, is less appealing. Anaya is a child at heart; his instinctive feelings ally him more with the *llano* than the *barrio.* And they relate him to the child in all of us.

We are reminded again of the rite of passage from innocence to the world of rational knowledge. Few of us achieve this passage without extinguishing the creative fire ignited in us by the magic of words. That fire still burns brightly in Anaya. He has learned to use the tools of his trade as an associate professor at the University, while founding the Rio Grande Writers Association, organizing writers' conferences and workshops, lecturing often throughout the country, and writing articles, reviews, and short stories.

Anaya today is wholeheartedly committed to expanding public awareness of Chicano cultural values. Yet, as I have ventured to say, his great appeal extends beyond this ethnic and geographic field. A close look at a fourth book, of which he is part author, may suggest why. It is *Cuentos: Tales from the Hispanic Southwest* (1980), a bilingual collection of old folktales first compiled and transcribed by Juan B. Rael, adapted into Spanish by José Griego y Maestas, and reworked into English versions by Anaya. How universal are these old, old tales. They span the centuries from the Moors and Jews in Spain, to the Spaniards in Mexico, whence they were brought to the Southwest by Spanish and Mexican settlers, picking up on the way native Indian myths and legends that still infuse old dances and ceremonies of the Pueblo Indians in New Mexico. Folktales of Death and Luck, kings and burros, men who knew the language of birds and animals; of Malinche, El Abuelo, and El Toro, too. These were the stories orally told to Anaya as a child, the rich ore body he has mined so well in his novels. Tales of a time when mankind itself was in childhood, their appeal today is not limited to children or Spanish-speaking adults. And we English readers are indebted not only to Anaya's graceful rendering of them into our modern idiom, but his talent to evoke the wonder and mystery within us all.

What I'm suggesting is that we can't label Anaya as solely a successful Chicano writer. He is developing into a major American writer expressing universal values through his own medium.

His perspectives are still expanding, like those of all of us in this shrinking one-world. The values of all cultural entities, be they civilizations, races, nations, or isolated cultural entities like those of the Chicanos, are embraced within the universal domain of the human spirit, which knows no boundaries. What it has felt and divined in ancient Egypt and Mesoamerica, in the American Southwest and Santa Rosa, and what it is feeling and divining everywhere today in this tragic world of change, is essentially the same. It is that inner urge toward realization of our common humanness and its inherent harmony with the entire universe.

In Commemoration
One Million Volumes

RUDOLFO A. ANAYA

A MILLION VOLUMES.

A magic number.

A million books to read, to look at, to hold in one's hand, to learn, to dream. . . .

I have always known there were at least a million stars. In the summer evenings when I was a child, we, all the children of the neighborhood, sat outside under the stars and listened to the stories of the old ones, los viejitos. The stories of the old people taught us to wonder and imagine. Their adivinanzas induced the stirring of our first questioning, our early learning.

I remember my grandfather raising his hand and pointing to the swirl of the Milky Way which swept over us. Then he would whisper his favorite riddle:

> Hay un hombre con tanto dinero
> Que no lo puede contar
> Una mujer con una sábana tan grande
> Que no la puede doblar.

> There is a man with so much money
> He cannot count it
> A woman with a bedspread so large
> She cannot fold it

We knew the million stars were the coins of the Lord, and the heavens were the bedspread of his mother, and in our minds the sky was a million miles wide. A hundred million. Infinite. Stuff for the imagination. And what was more important, the teachings of the old ones made us see that we were bound to the infinity of that cosmic dance of life which swept around us. Their teachings created in us a thirst for knowledge. Can this library with its million volumes bestow that same inspiration?

I was fortunate to have had those old and wise viejitos as guides into the world of nature and knowledge. They taught me with their stories; they taught me the magic of words. Now the words lie captured in ink, but the magic is still there, the power inherent in each volume. Now with book in hand we can participate in the wisdom of mankind.

Each person moves from innocence through rites of passage into the knowledge of the world, and so I entered the world of school in search of the magic in the words. The sounds were no longer the soft sounds of Spanish which my grandfather spoke; the words were in English, and with each new awareness came my first steps toward a million volumes. I, who was used to reading my oraciones en español while I sat in the kitchen and answered the litany to the slap of my mother's tortillas, I now stumbled from sound to word to groups of words, head throbbing, painfully aware that each new sound took me deeper into the maze of the new language. Oh, how I clutched the hands of my new guides then!

Learn, my mother encouraged me, learn. Be as wise as your grandfather. He could speak many languages. He could speak to the birds and the animals of the field.

Yes, I remember the cuentos of my grandfather, the stories of the people. Words are a way, he said, they hold joy, and they are a deadly power if misused. I clung to each syllable which lisped from his tobacco-stained lips. That was the winter the snow came, he would say, it piled high and we lost many sheep and cattle, and the trees groaned and broke with its weight. I looked across the llano and saw the raging blizzard, the awful destruction of that winter which was imbedded in our people's mind.

And the following summer, he would say, the grass of the llano grew so high we couldn's see the top of the sheep. And I would look and see what was once clean and pure and green. I could see a million sheep and the pastores caring for them, as I now care for the million words that pasture in my mind.

But a million books? How can we see a million books? I don't mean just the books lining the shelves here at the University of New Mexico Library, not just the fine worn covers, the intriguing titles; how can we see the worlds that lie waiting in each book? A million worlds. A million million worlds. And the beauty of it is that each world is related to the next, as was taught to us by the old ones. Perhaps it is easier for a child to see. Perhaps it is easier for a child to ask: how many stars are there in the sky? How many leaves in the trees of the river? How many blades of grass in the llano? How many dreams in a night of dreams?

So I worked my way into the world of books, but here is the paradox, a book at once quenches the thirst of the imagination and ignites new fires. I learned that as I visited the library of my childhood, the Santa Rosa library. It was only a dusty room in those days, a room sitting atop the town's fire department, which was comprised of one dilapidated fire truck used by the town's volunteers only in the direst emergencies. But in that small room I found my shelter and retreat. If there were a hundred books there we were fortunate, but to me there were a million volumes. I trembled in awe when I first entered that library, because I realized that if the books held as much magic as the words of the old ones, then indeed this was a room full of power.

Miss Pansy, the librarian, became my new guide. She fed me books as any mother would nurture her child. She brought me book after book, and I consumed them all. Saturday afternoons disappeared as the time of day dissolved into the time of distant worlds. In a world that occupied most of my other schoolmates with games, I took the time to read. I was a librarian's dream. My tattered library card was my ticket into the same worlds my grandfather had known, worlds of magic that fed the imagination.

Late in the afternoon, when I was satiated with reading, when I could no longer hold in my soul the characters that crowded there, I heard the call of the llano, the real world of my father's ranchito, the solid, warm world of my mother's kitchen. Then to the surprise and bewilderment of Miss Pansy, I would rush out and race down the streets of our town, books tucked under my shirt, in my pockets, clutched tightly to my breast. Mad with the insanity of books, I would cross the river to get home, shouting my crazy challenge even at la Llorona, and that poor spirit of so many frightening cuentos would wither and withdraw. She was no match for me.

Those of you who have felt the same exhilaration from reading—or from love—will know about what I'm speaking. Alas, the people of the town could only shake their heads and pity my mother. At least one of her sons was a bit touched. Perhaps they were right, for few will trade a snug reality to float on words to other worlds.

And now there are a million volumes for us to read here at the University of New Mexico Library. Books on every imaginable subject, in every field, a history of the thought of the world which we must keep free of censorship, because we treasure our freedoms. It is the word *freedom* which eventually must reflect what this collection, or the collection of any library, is all about. We know that as we preserve and use the literature of all cultures, we preserve and regenerate our own. The old ones knew and taught me this. They eagerly read the few newspapers that were available. They kept their diaries, they wrote décimas and cuentos, and they survived on their oral stories and traditions.

Another time, another library. I entered Albuquerque High School Library prepared to study, because that's where we spent our study time. For better or for worse, I received my first contracts as a writer there. It was a place where budding lovers spent most of their time writing notes to each other, and when my friends who didn't have the gift of words found out I could turn a phrase I quickly had all the business I could do. I wrote poetic love notes for a dime apiece and thus worked my way through high school. And there were fringe benefits, because the young women knew very well who was writing the sweet words, and many a heart I was supposed to capture fell in love with me. And so, a library is also a place where love begins.

A library should be the heart of a city. With its storehouse of knowledge, it liberates, informs, teaches, and enthralls. A library indeed should be the cultural center of any city. Amidst the bustle of work and commerce, the great libraries of the world have provided a sanctuary where scholars and common man alike come to enlarge and clarify knowledge, to read and reflect in quiet solitude.

I knew a place like this, I spent many hours in the old library on Central Avenue and Edith Street. But my world was growing, and quite by accident I wandered up the hill to enroll in the University of New Mexico. And what a surprise lay in store for me. The libraries of my childhood paled in comparison to this new wealth of books housed in Zimmerman Library. Here there were stack after stack of books, and ample space and time to wander aimlessly in this labyrinth of new frontiers.

I had known the communal memory of my people through the newspapers and few books my grandfather read to me and through the rich oral tradition handed down by the old ones; now I discovered the collective memory of all mankind at my fingertips. I had only to reach for the books that laid all history bare. Here I could converse with the writers from every culture on earth, old and new, and at the same time I began my personal odyssey, which would add a few books to the collection which in 1981 would come to house a million volumes.

Those were exciting times. Around me swirled the busy world of the university, in many respects an alien world. Like many fellow undergraduates, I sought refuge in the library. My haven during those student university years was the reading room of the west wing of the old library. There I found peace. The carved vigas decorating the ceiling, the solid wooden tables and chairs and the warm adobe color of the stucco were things with which I was familiar. There I felt comfortable. With books scattered around me, I could read and doze and dream. I took my breaks in the warm sun of the portal, where I ate my tortilla sandwiches, which I carried in my brown paper bag. There, with friends, I sipped coffee as we talked of changing the world and exchanged idealistic dreams.

That is a rich and pleasant time in my memory. No matter

how far across the world I find myself in the future, how deep in the creation of worlds with words, I shall keep the simple and poignant memories of those days. The sun set golden on the ocher walls, and the green pine trees and the blue spruce, sacred trees to our people, whispered in the breeze. I remembered my grandfather meeting with the old men of the village in the resolana of one of the men's homes, or against the wall of the church on Sundays, and I remembered the things they said. Later, alone, dreaming against the sun-warmed wall of the library, I continued that discourse in my mind.

Yes, the library is a place where people should gather. It is a place for research, reading, and for the quiet fomentation of ideas, but because it houses the collective memory of our race, it should also be a place where present issues are discussed and debated and researched in order for us to gain the knowledge and insight to create a better future. The library should be a warm place that reflects the needs and aspirations of the people.

The University of New Mexico Library didn't have a million volumes when I first haunted its corridors of stacks, but now these million volumes are available. The library has grown. Sometimes I get lost when I wander through it, and I cannot help but wonder if there are students around me who are also lost. Is there someone who will guide them through this storehouse of knowledge? A labyrinth can be a frightening place without a guide, and perhaps that is why I have written about some of the guides who took my hand and helped me. It is important to celebrate not only the acquisition of the millionth volume, but to rededicate ourselves to the service of our community, which is an integral part of the history of this library. I am confident that the library will continue to grow and to be an example to other libraries. Service to the community is indeed our most important endeavor.

This millionth volume marks a momentous step in the process of growth of the University of New Mexico Library. This commemorative volume celebrates that step. In the wisest cultures of the world, entry into adulthood is a time of celebration, it is a time for dancing and the thanksgiving. And that is what we, the staff of the library, the scholars of the university, the students, the friends and the people from the community come to celebrate this year. We gather not only to celebrate growth, but also to note the excellence of archives in many fields, to acknowledge the change that has met the demands of the present and needs of the future, and to honor the service provided to all of the people who come here to read, to dream, to recreate.

So, let us celebrate this rite of passage. It is a time to flex our muscles and be proud. We have come a long way from the first collection, and we will continue to build. I would like to list the names of all the people who have worked to bring us this moment, but since that is impossible it is the intent of this personal essay to thank those people.

This reminiscence through libraries I have known and dreamed in is a thanks to those librarians whose efforts helped to establish this library. In their spirit we will offer help to each person who comes through the doors of this library in that curious but inalienable right to search for knowledge.

En Conmemoración
Un Millón de Volúmenes

TRANSLATED BY MATILDE J. FARREN

UN MILLÓN DE VOLÚMENES.
Una cifra mágica.
Un millón de libros para leer, para mirar, para sentir en la mano, para aprender, para soñar.

Siempre supe que había por lo menos un millón de estrellas. En las tardecitas de verano cuando yo era niño, nosotros, los chicos de la vecindad, nos sentábamos bajo las estrellas a escuchar los cuentos de los viejitos. Los cuentos de los viejos nos enseñaron a maravillarnos, a imaginar. Sus adivinanzas incitaron nuestras primeras preguntas, sus palabras fueron nuestro primer aprendizaje.

Me acuerdo de mi abuelo, señalando con su mano en alto el remolino envolvente de la Vía Láctea. Luego murmuraba su adivinanza preferida:

> Hay un hombre con tanto dinero
> que no lo puede contar.
> Una mujer con una sábana tan grande
> que no la puede doblar.

Todos sabíamos que el millón de estrellas eran las monedas del Señor, y los cielos la sábana de su Madre, y en nuestras mentes el cielo era de un millón de millas de ancho. Cien millones. Infinito. Alimento para la imaginación. Y, más importante aún, las enseñanzas de los viejos nos hacían ver que estábamos ligados a la infinitud de la danza cósmica de la vida que nos envolvía. Sus enseñanzas crearon en nosotros la sed de aprender. ¿Sería posible que esta biblioteca con su millón de volúmenes, despertara la misma inspiración?

Yo tuve la suerte de haber tenido a aquellos viejitos sabios como guías en el mundo de la naturaleza y del conocimiento. Me enseñaron con sus cuentos, me enseñaron con la magia de las palabras. Ahora las palabras son prisioneras de la tinta, pero la magia sigue allí, el poder inherente a cada volumen. Ahora, libro en mano, podemos ser partícipes de la sabiduría de la humanidad.

Toda persona pasa de la inocencia, por ritos de transición, al conocimiento del mundo; así entré yo al mundo de la escuela, en busca de la magia encerrada en la palabra. Los sonidos ya no eran los suaves sonidos del español que hablaba mi abuelo; las palabras eran en inglés, y con cada nuevo descubrimiento se encaminaban mis pasos hacia un millón de volúmenes. Yo, acostumbrado a leer mis oraciones en español, sentado en la cocina practicando el catecismo al ritmo de las palmadas de las tortillas de mi madre, ahora tropezaba del sonido, a la palabra, a grupos de palabras, con un martilleo en la cabeza, con dolorosa conciencia de que con cada nuevo sonido me internaba más profundamente en el laberinto del nuevo idioma. ¡Oh, cómo me aferraba entonces a la mano de mis nuevos guías!

Aprende, me alentaba mi madre, aprende para que seas tan sabio como tu abuelo. Él hablaba muchos idiomas. Él podía hablar con los pájaros y con los animales del campo.

Sí, recuerdo los cuentos de mi abuelo, las historias de la gente. Las palabras son una herramienta, decía él, encierran ventura, pero tienen un poder mortífero si se las usa mal. Yo me quedaba pendiente de hasta la última sílaba que él ceceaba con sus labios manchados de tabaco. Ese fue el invierno en que llegó la nieve, contaba él, se apiló alta y perdimos mucho ganado y ovejas, y los árboles crujían y se rompían con el peso de la nieve. Yo miraba al llano y veía la furiosa tormenta, la terrible destrucción de aquel invierno grabado en la memoria de nuestra gente.

El verano siguiente, continuaba mi abuelo, los pastos del llano crecieron tan altos que no veíamos los lomos de las ovejas. Yo miraba y veía lo que una vez fue limpio y puro y verde. Yo veía un millón de ovejas y los pastores que las apacentaban, así como yo ahora apaciento el millón de palabras que pastan en mi mente.

Empero ¿un millón de libros? ¿Cómo podemos ver un millón de libros? No me refiero solamente a los libros alineados en los estantes de la Universidad de Nuevo México, o a las finas cubiertas gastadas, los fascinantes títulos, o a la visión que nos dan de los mundos que yacen a la espera en cada volumen. Un millón de mundos. Un millón de millones de mundos. Lo bueno es que cada mundo se relaciona con el siguiente, como nos enseñaron los viejitos. Tal vez sea más fácil de ver para un niño. Tal vez le sea más fácil preguntar cuántas estrellas hay en el cielo. ¿Cuántas hojas en los árboles a la orilla del río? ¿Cuántas briznas de pasto en el llano? ¿Cuántos sueños en una noche de sueños?

Así me abrí camino en el mundo de los libros, pero aquí está la paradoja. Un libro sacia la sed de la imaginación al mismo tiempo que enciende nuevos fuegos. Eso lo aprendí al visitar la biblioteca de mi niñez, la biblioteca de Santa Rosa. En aquellos días no era más que una sala polvorienta, una sala en los altos del cuartel de bomberos, compuesto de una vieja autobomba que los voluntarios del pueblo usaban únicamente en casos de suma urgencia. Pero en esa pequeña sala yo encontré mi refugio y mi retiro. Puede que con suerte hubiera habido cien libros en la biblioteca, pero para mí era un millón de volúmenes. Temblé con reverencia la primera vez que entré a aquella sala, pues me di cuenta de que si los libros encerraban tanta magia como las palabras de los ancianos, entonces ésa debería ser una sala poderosísima.

La señorita Violeta, la bibliotecaria, fue mi nueva guía. Me nutría con libros como cualquier madre alimentaría a su hijo. Me traía libro tras libro, yo los consumía todos. La tarde del sábado desaparecía mientras el tiempo real se disolvía en el tiempo de mundos lejanos. En un mundo en el que la mayoría de mis compañeros se entretenía jugando, yo leía. Yo era el sueño de toda bibliotecaria. Mi ajada tarjeta de socio era mi entrada a los mismos mundos que mi abuelo había conocido, mundos de magia que nutrían la imaginación.

Ya tarde, ahíto de lectura, cuando ya no podía contener en mi alma los personajes que en ella se apiñaban, oía la voz del llano, el mundo real del ranchito de mi padre, el sólido y cálido mundo de la cocina de mi madre. Entonces, para sorpresa e incomprensión de la señorita Violeta, me alejaba corriendo por las calles del pueblo, los libros metidos en la camisa, en los bolsillos, apretados contra mi pecho. Loco con la locura de los libros, cruzaba el río para llegar a mi casa, con mi delirante desafío que no respetaba ni a La Llorona, y ese pobre espíritu de tantos cuentos aterradores se marchitaba y desaparecía. No era rival para mí.

Los que hayan sentido la misma alegría con la lectura—o con el amor—sabrán de qué hablo. La gente del pueblo no podía sino menear la cabeza y compadecer a mi madre. Ay ay, por lo menos uno de sus hijos era un poquito tocado. Tal vez tuvieran razón, pues pocos serán los que abandonen la sólida realidad para flotar sobre palabras hacia mundos desconocidos.

Y ahora hay un millón de volúmenes para leer aquí en la biblioteca de la Universidad de Nuevo México. Libros que tratan de toda materia imaginable, en todos los campos, una historia del pensamiento universal que debemos conservar libre de la censura, porque valoramos encarecidamente nuestras libertades. Es la palabra libertad la que debe reflejar el sentido fundamental de esta colección, o la colección de cualquier biblioteca. Sabemos que mientras pensamos y usamos la literatura de cualquier cultura, preservamos y regeneramos la propia. Los viejitos lo sabían y me lo enseñaron. Ávidamente leían los pocos periódicos disponibles. Mantenían sus diarios, escribían décimas y cuentos, y sobrevivían con sus tradiciones e historias orales.

Otros tiempos, otra biblioteca. Entré a la biblioteca de la Escuela Secundaria de Albuquerque dispuesto a estudiar, puesto que allí pasábamos las horas de estudio. Para bien o para mal, allí fue donde recibí mis primeros contratos como escritor. Aquel era un lugar donde los jóvenes en los albores del amor pasaban el tiempo escribiéndose galanteos. Cuando mis amigos menos inspirados descubrieron que yo podía componer una copla, pronto tuve todo el trabajo que quise. Escribía poemas de amor por diez centavos, y así trabajé toda la escuela secundaria. Además el trabajo tenía sus beneficios, pues las jóvenes sabían muy bien quién era el autor de las dulces palabras, y más de un corazón a quien el poema debía capturar se enamoraba de mí. Por lo tanto, la biblioteca también es el lugar donde comienza el amor.

La biblioteca debería ser el corazón de la ciudad, con su caudal de conocimientos que libera, enseña, informa, y cautiva. La biblioteca debería por cierto ser el centro cultural de toda ciudad. En el fárrago del comercio y el trabajo, las grandes bibliotecas del mundo ofrecen un refugio donde tanto el estudioso como el hombre de la calle vienen a ampliar y aclarar el conocimiento, a leer y reflexionar en tranquila soledad.

En Conmemoración: Un Millón de Volúmenes

Yo conocí un lugar de estos; yo pasé muchas horas en la vieja biblioteca de la esquina de la calle Edith y Avenida Central. Mi mundo crecía, y en forma casi accidental encaminé mis pasos hacia la colina, a inscribirme en la Universidad de Nuevo México. ¡Qué sorpresa me esperaba allí! Las bibliotecas de mi niñez palidecían con el caudal de libros que moraban en la biblioteca Zimmerman. Aquí había estante tras estante de libros, y abundante espacio y tiempo para vagar sin rumbo en este laberinto de nuevos horizontes.

Yo había conocido la memoria comunitaria de mi gente a través de los pocos libros y periódicos que mi abuelo me había leido; a través de la rica tradición oral transmitida por los ancianos, ahora descubría la memoria colectiva de la humanidad entera al alcance de mi mano. No tenía más que estirar la mano para conseguir los libros que me revelarían toda la historia. Aquí podía yo conversar con los escritores de todas las culturas de la tierra, antiguas y modernas, y al mismo tiempo comencé mi odisea personal que añadiría unos pocos libros a la colección que en 1981 alcanzaría el millón de volúmenes.

Aquellos fueron tiempos de feliz entusiasmo. A mi alrededor se arremolinaba el activo mundo de la universidad, en muchos sentidos un mundo extraño. Como muchos compañeros subgraduados, busqué refugio en la biblioteca. Mi abrigo durante esos años de estudiante universitario estaba en la sala de lectura del ala occidental de la vieja biblioteca. Allí encontré paz. Las vigas talladas que decoran el techo, las sólidas mesas y sillas de madera y el cálido color adobe de las paredes eran cosas familiares para mí. Allí me sentía cómodo. Con los libros desparramados a mi alrededor, podía leer, dormitar, y soñar. Mis recreos me los tomaba al cálido sol del portal, donde comía los sandwiches de tortilla de maiz que llevaba en mi bolsa de papel. Allí, con mis amigos, tomaba café a sorbitos mientras hablábamos de cambiar el mundo e intercambiábamos sueños idealistas.

Aquélla es una rica y agradable época en mis recuerdos. Aunque el futuro me lleve al otro extremo del mundo, no importa cuán profundamente inmerso me encuentre en la creación de otros mundos con palabras, siempre llevaré conmigo el sencillo y conmovedor recuerdo de aquellos días. El sol poniente era de oro sobre las paredes ocres; los verdes pinos y el cedro azul, árboles sagrados para nuestra gente, silbaban en la brisa. Me acordaba de mi abuelo reunido con los viejos del pueblo en la resolana de la casa de uno de ellos, o apoyado contra la pared de la iglesia los domingos, y me acordaba de las cosas que decían. Más tarde, solo, reclinado contra la cálida pared de la biblioteca entibiada por el sol, continuaba la plática en mi mente.

Sí, la biblioteca debería ser un lugar de reunión. Es cierto que es un lugar para la investigación, para la lectura, para el tranquilo fomento de las ideas, pero, ya que aloja la memoria colectiva de nuestra raza, también debería ser un lugar donde los problemas presentes se debaten, se investigan y se discuten, para que podamos adquirir el conocimiento y el discernimiento necesarios para construir un futuro mejor. La biblioteca debería ser un lugar cálido, que refleje las necesidades y aspiraciones del pueblo.

La biblioteca de la Universidad de Nuevo México no tenía un millón de volúmenes cuando yo comencé a frecuentar sus corredores y pasillos, pero ahora ese millón de volúmenes existe. La biblioteca ha crecido. A veces me pierdo en mis vagabundeos por allí, y me pregunto si no habrá estudiantes a mi alrededor que también estén perdidos. ¿Habrá alguien que los guíe por esta mina de conocimientos? Un laberinto sin guía puede ser un lugar aterrador, y tal vez sea por eso que he escrito sobre los guías que me tomaron de la mano y me ayudaron. Es importante celebrar no sólo la adquisición del millonésimo volumen, sino también la re-dedicación al servicio de nuestra comunidad, que es parte integral de la historia de esta biblioteca. Confío en que seguirá creciendo y presentando un ejemplo a otras bibliotecas. Por cierto, el servicio a la comunidad es nuestra misión más importante.

El millonésimo volumen marca un paso trascendental en el proceso de crecimiento de la biblioteca de la Universidad de Nuevo México. Este volumen conmemorativo celebra ese paso. En las culturas más sabias del mundo, la entrada a la edad adulta es motivo de celebración, de danzas y de acciones de gracias. Esto es lo que nosotros, el personal de la biblioteca, profesores y estudiantes, amigos y representantes de la comunidad, venimos a celebrar este año. Nos reunimos no sólo para celebrar el conocimiento, sino también para señalar la excelencia de los archivos en muchos campos, para reconocer el cambio que satisface las exigencias del presente y las necesidades del futuro, y para rendir honor al servicio prestado a todas las personas que vienen aquí a leer, a soñar, a pasar un rato creativo.

Celebremos esta ceremonia de transición. Es el momento de reconocer nuestra fuerza y nuestro orgullo. Hemos avanzado mucho desde nuestra primera colección, y seguiremos construyendo. Me gustaría mencionar los nombres de todas las personas que han colaborado para llegar a donde estamos, pero ya que eso es imposible, es intención de este ensayo personal expresarles mi gratitud a todos. Estas reminiscencias sobre bibliotecas que he conocido y en las que he soñado, son un agradecimiento a todos aquellos bibliotecarios cuyos esfuerzos contribuyeron al establecimiento de esta biblioteca. Con el mismo espíritu de ellos, ofreceremos ayuda a todo el que pase por estas puertas, con ese curioso pero inalienable derecho a la búsqueda del conocimiento.

The Achievement of Rudolfo A. Anaya

ANTONIO MÁRQUEZ

THE HOMAGE TO Rudolfo Anaya comes at an appropriate time. Recently, *The New York Times Book Review* belatedly granted him national status. Moreover, Anaya's work is on the verge of international recognition. The growing interest in Anaya and other Chicano writers in Latin America and Europe, attended by the expected translations of *Bless Me, Ultima* into German and Polish, opens new vistas for Chicano literature. Just as *Bless Me, Ultima* (and Tomás Rivera's *Y No Se Lo Tragó La Tierra*) formed the vanguard of modern Chicano prose, Anaya's work is at the vanguard that promises to liberate Chicano literature from the confines of "ethnic" or "regionalist" literature. It is befitting for Anaya to receive the honor and the task of leading Chicano literature into the canons of world literature. He is the most acclaimed and the most popular and universal Chicano writer, and one of the most influential voices in contemporary Chicano literature.

Anaya's literary career has been energetically diverse:

novelist, essayist, folklorist, short-story writer, and playwright. Not slighting this admirable diversity, Anaya's major contribution has been as a novelist, and his reputation and achievement largely rest on *Bless Me, Ultima, Heart of Aztlán,* and *Tortuga.* Therefore, this survey focuses on Anaya's novels. It is a conspectus that will exclude critical examination of the plots, characters, folklore, legends, extensive symbolism, and other particulars that animate his novels. An accompanying bibliography notes the numerous articles, theses, and dissertations that have provided exegeses on these aspects of Anaya's fiction. In fact, concomitant with his role as the most acclaimed Chicano writer, his work (especially *Bless Me, Ultima*) has inspired the largest body of criticism in contemporary Chicano literature. This essay, then, is a general assessment of Anaya's position in Chicano literature, the critical reception of his work, and the nature of his achievement and reputation.

It was *Bless Me, Ultima* (1972) that vaulted Anaya to a stellar position in Chicano literature and a significant place in American literature. The subsequent novels, *Heart of Aztlán* (1976) and *Tortuga* (1979), solidified his reputation. To assess the significance of Anaya's work one must first consider its place in Chicano literary history. The appearance of *Bless Me, Ultima* was auspicious and rather startling. It stood in stark contrast to the shrill polemics that emerged from the political cauldron of the 1960s and attempted to pass for literature. *Bless Me, Ultima,* a muted and subtle work that dissuaded politics, projected reams of symbols and archetypes, and fused realism and fantasy, demonstrated that it was a painstakingly crafted novel. There appeared in the often woolly perimeters of Chicano fiction a singularly accomplished novel. To appreciate this accomplishment one only has to view his predecessors. José Antonio Villarreal's *Pocho,* Raymond Barrio's *The Plum Plum Pickers,* and Richard Vásquez's *Chicano,* for example, were important literary expressions of Chicano life, but they were marred as novels. All too often stilted and amateurish, they lacked novelistic invention or artistry. In the early 1970s two works appeared that marked a significant break from formulaic "social protest literature." These two works, Rivera's *Y No Se Lo Tragó La Tierra* and Anaya's *Bless Me, Ultima,* initiated the maturity and diversification of contemporary Chicano fiction. Quite different in theme and form, they were distinguished by their structural complexity and innovative exploration of Chicano life. Informed with the experimental techniques of William Faulkner and especially of Juan Rulfo, Rivera brought an eviscerating realism and existentialist thematics to Chicano fiction. On the other hand, Anaya's novel opened new vistas with its richly poetic vein and mythic configurations. Equally important, they brought a greater honesty and authenticity to the portrayal of Chicano life and countered stereotypic literature on the Chicano. *Bless Me, Ultima* forcefully dramatized that "Chicanos are not simple, fun-loving, tradition-bound, lovable non-achievers or other mythical stereotypes such as those produced by John Steinbeck, but, rather, complex individuals like those found in any society."[1] In a similar vein, Daniel Testa, who has provided the most astute criticism on *Bless Me, Ultima,* concluded his critical study with praise for Anaya's large accomplishment and promising talent: "As a creative writer and spokesman for the Hispano-mestizo minority, who for too long has struggled in the backwaters of American life, Anaya gives every indication of invigorating the cultural growth of his people and verifying the existence of an inner force and power in their daily lives."[2]

Although some critics were irritated by its "affectations" and "artistic naivete," *Bless Me, Ultima* was generally well-received and enthusiastically acclaimed in some quarters. It was deservedly praised for its fine storytelling, superb craftsmanship, and the artistic and philosophic dignity that it brought to Chicano literature. However, the joy of discovery often took injudicious turns; some critics celebrated *Bless Me, Ultima as* "an American classic" and carelessly and erroneously placed Anaya among Faulkner and Joyce. Fortunately, most assessments of *Bless Me, Ultima* were sensible and gave the work and its author their due worth. Martin Bucco exemplifies the judicious criticism:

> To be sure, if Anaya is not a world voice, he is at least a valuable new one, gifted and youthful, his creative consciousness sug-

1. Rolando Hinojosa, "Mexican-American Literature: Toward An Identification," *Books Abroad,* 49, No. 3 (Summer 1975): 422-30.

2. Daniel Testa, "Extensive/Intensive Dimensionality in Anaya's *Bless Me, Ultima," Latin American Literary Review,* V, No. 10 (Spring-Summer 1977): 70–78.

gesting, establishing, creating . . . the serious Mexican-American regional novel need not atrophy simply because it does not coincide with mass taste or with the complex art of Joyce, Gide, and Faulkner.[3]

The most common refrain was that *Bless Me, Ultima* "achieved something that few pieces of Chicano literature have; that is, simply, that it stands by itself as a novel, with the 'Chicano' added later. . . ."[4] The emphasis on *Bless Me, Ultima's* primary achievement as a novel and its secondary trait of ethnicity is an appropriate criterion. Ultimately, the novel's success rests on Anaya's imaginative mythopoesis and his careful and loving attention to the craft of fiction. The latter quality leads to a larger issue. Anaya from the start has seen himself, and rightly so, as an artist. He has vigorously made clear that he is not an apologist, polemicist, or literary ideologue, and he has frequently spoken out against the "politicization" of art: "I think any kind of description or dictation to the artist as a creative person will ruin his creative impulse. . . . The best writers will deal with social responsibility and the welfare of the people indirectly—as opposed to direct political statement or dogma."[5]

3. Martin Bucco, "A Review of *Bless Me, Ultima,*" *Southwestern American Literature,* 2, No. 3 (Winter 1972): 153–54.

4. Dyan Donnelly, "Finding a Home in the World," *Bilingual Review,* 1, No. 1 (January-April 1974): 113–18.

5. David Johnson and David Apodaca, "Myth and the Writer: A Conversation with Rudolfo Anaya," *New America,* 3, No. 3 (Spring 1979): 76–85.

Anaya's aestheticism and his avoidance of doctrinaire politics have been the major targets of his detractors. And his detractors, mostly academic critics and ideologues of the marxist stripe, found ample ground in *Heart of Aztlán* for their contentions. The general attack is that Anaya's archaism and myth-making are vague abstractions that have no bearing on existing and pressing issues. In a recent panel discussion with other Chicano writers and academics, Anaya offered this explanation of his mythopoesis:

> I define myth as the truth in the heart. It is the truth that you have carried, that we as human beings have carried all of our history, going back to the cave, pushing it back to the sea. It seems to me that what happens at a certain time with people is that in order to come to a new conscious awareness they need to separate necessarily from a social, political context.[6]

Anaya subsequently took the critical brunt of the colloquium. One participant voiced a common complaint about Anaya's fiction: "I think that his idea of truth in the heart is very, very abstract." Another participant was rankled by the lack of practicality in Anaya's myth-making: ". . . looking back to the man with ultimate wisdom . . . won't answer the problem that's facing us directly and that's never answered." Alurista, a major Chicano poet and Anaya's most testy adversary in this exchange, questioned Anaya's archaism and

6. "Mitólogos y Mitómanos," *Maize: Xicano Art and Literature Notebooks,* 4, Nos. 3–4 (Spring-Summer 1981): 6–23.

concluded: "Necesitamos un mito más racional que confronte las necesidades contemporáneas, y que confronte el enemigo del espíritu del hombre [We need a more rational myth that will confront contemporary necessities, and that will confront the enemy of the human spirit.]"[7] This confrontation is used as an example of the numerous occasions where Anaya has been taken to task and prompted to defend his work. One can plausibly assume that Anaya by now is weary of these polemical confrontations and indifferent to the criticism that argues that he has failed to become a "committed" and "relevant" Chicano writer.

The controversy found specific grounds in *Heart of Aztlán*. The critical reception was divided and often delusive: its champions were charmed by the mythic substructure and poetic correspondences, but ignored its technical discrepancies; its detractors damned the confusing mixture of politics and metaphysics, but ignored the frequent moments of lyrical and poignant introspection. Some readers cloyed the novel and made heady assessments: "In *Heart of Aztlán* a prose-writer with the soul of a poet, and a dedication to his calling that only the greatest artists ever sustain—is on an important track, the right one, the only one."[8] On the other hand, some critics were vexed by the novel's diffused narrative line and vague morality:

7. Ibid., passim.
8. Karl Kopp, "A Review of Heart of Aztlán," *La Confluencia,* 1, Nos. 3–4 (July 1977): 62–63.

Can insight into the existence of a spiritual bond destroy oppression and end exploitation? Can the feeling of a shared communal soul destroy the chains of steel that bind the people? Is
there not some other ingredient necessary in addition to a
spiritual feeling of love? Has contact with the myths provided
a real tool to correct social injustice?[9]

There was much blather over Anaya's exotic metaphysics
and fuzzy political notions, but very few readers pinpointed
the chief failing of *Heart of Aztlán*. The crux of the matter
was suggested by Bruce-Novoa in a brief preface to an interview with Anaya: "*Ultima* produced expectations that *Heart
of Aztlán* did not satisfy. Not that the introduction of
blatantly political topics is a fault in and of itself—no, it is a
matter of the craftsmanship, not of the themes, and *Heart,*
for whatever reason, is less polished, less accomplished."[10]
Precisely, the novel's detriment was its lack of craftsmanship.
Heart of Aztlán stands out as a blemish in the Anaya canon
because its disjointed and amorphous style contrasts with the
meticulous, controlled, and carefully executed prose of
Anaya's other works. Ostensibly, it was an experiment that
sought to combine mythic elements and a socioeconomic
theme. It attempts to balance and form a correlation between
the myth of Aztlán (presented in numerous symbols and
archetypes) and barrio life in Albuquerque in the 1950s

9. María López Hoffman, "Myth and Reality: Heart of Aztlán,"
De Colores, 5, Nos. 1–2 (1980): 111–14.

10. Bruce-Novoa, *Chicano Authors: Inquiry by Interview* (Austin:
University of Texas Press, 1980), p. 184.

(presented in realistic details of socioeconomic conditions and the labor struggles of the time). But it is a literary mixed-bag rather than a cohesive work of fiction. Apparently, Anaya placed himself in a difficult novelistic stratagem in trying to work two discordant plots and themes. Anaya has commented on the technical problems involved in transforming Clemente from a drunken wastrel to a spiritual visionary that leads a labor struggle armed with love and mysticism:

> It's most difficult, because he's caught up in a very realistic setting and then how in hell do you take him into his visionary trip that I attempted to do with Clemente. I suppose I could have done it in a dream, I could have done it in some kind of revelation, and I chose to do it instead through Crispín and the old woman, the keeper of the rock.[11]

Anaya's telling comments on the "visionary trip" that leads to the novel's rather forced resolution suggest that Anaya was not confident or totally clear about the execution of the novel. Culling this candid moment of auto-criticism, Anaya offered a more telling admission that shed light on his most common liability: his occasional rhetorical excesses and cutesy mannerisms. He explains his playful manner:

> I get a kick out of doing things that I know people will respond to, especially critics. In *Heart of Aztlán* I did something that was really too cutesy. . . 'The sun sucked the holy waters of the river,

11. "Myth and the Writer: A Conversation with Rudolfo Anaya," 82.

and the turtle bowl sky ripped open with dark thunder and fell
upon the land. South of Aztlán the golden bear drank his fill
and tasted the sweet fragrance of the drowned man's blood. That
evening he bedded down with the turtle's sisters and streaked
their virgin robes with virgin blood. . . . Oh wash my song into
the dead man's soul, he cried, and soak his marrow dry.' That's
part of that. I get carried away.[12]

Apart from the convoluted narration, Anaya touches on a
pointed issue. All too often, he is "cutesy" and "gets carried away" in purple prose.

The critical reception of *Tortuga* is less defined. At the
present, the criticism on Anaya's third novel consists of a
scattering of reviews. So far the reception of *Tortuga* has
been favorable. The cursory reviews have noted the strong
narrative line, the striking realism, and the novel's powerful
theme. However, the connecting elements in the trilogy
and Anaya's maturation have not been considered. Foremost, there is an integrity and cohesiveness to *Tortuga* that
were lacking in *Heart of Aztlán*. Apart from containing the
rudiments of Anaya's fiction—a mythopoeic cluster of images
and symbols, it discloses sharper insight and accommodation
of realistic situations. Notably, Anaya returns to first-person
narrative point of view, which seems to be more conformable
to his style. We can gather that Anaya in *Heart of Aztlán*
was stretching out and experimenting with new ways
of telling a story. The return to the narrative technique of

12. Ibid., 83.

The Achievement of Rudolfo A. Anaya

Bless Me, Ultima makes *Tortuga* a smooth and lucid novel which is free of the vagaries that made *Heart of Aztlán* less than successful. It can also be noted that Anaya returns to the exploration of "memory and imagination." These two elements gave *Bless Me, Ultima* a magical resonance. *Tortuga* achieves a similar effect with its Proustian overture and memory-laden images: "I awoke from a restless sleep. For a moment I couldn't remember where I was. . . Upon waking it was always the same; I tried to move but the paralysis held me firmly in its grip." (1) And later: "The words struck chords and a remembrance of things past would flood over me and in my imagination I would live in other times and other places. . . ."(54)

Tortuga, which has neither achieved the popularity and critical acclaim of *Bless Me, Ultima,* nor received the brick-bats leveled at *Heart of Aztlán,* is in several respects Anaya's most accomplished novel. True, there are still rhetorical excesses and inconsistencies in the lyrical voice. When measured and used to enlarge a character's sensibility, the lyricism is quite effective: "I followed her gaze and through her eyes I saw the beauty she described, the beauty I had not seen until that moment. The drabness of winter melted in the warm, spring light, and I saw the electric acid of life run through the short green fuses of the desert plants and crack through the dark buds to brush with strokes of lime the blooming land." (166) Here Anaya magically employs his poetic gift to catch an expressive moment. In the lesser moments, the lyrical manner is too self-conscious and rhapsodic. For example, at one point Anaya indulges in hackneyed Homeric metaphors:

> The daughter of the sun awoke to weave her blanket with pastel threads. Her soft, coral fingers worked swiftly to weave the bits of turquoise blue and mother of pearl into the silver sky. She had but a moment in which to weave the tapestry that covered her nakedness, because behind her the sun trumpeted, awoke roaring alive with fire and exploded into the sky, filling the desert with glorious light and scattering the mist of the river and the damp humours of the night. Dawn blushed and fled as the sun straddled the mountain, and the mountain groaned under the welcomed light. The earth trembled at the sight. (27)

At such moments, one wishes that Anaya had been more restrained. Happily, such passages are few and the greater part of the narrative is enriched with vibrant lyricism.

Moreover, *Tortuga* is the product of Anaya's increasing prowess as a novelist, and one can conjecture that Anaya esteems it as his best work. His third novel demonstrates, notwithstanding the discrepancy noted above, that Anaya has conscientiously worked at his craft. In brief, it is a more disciplined and carefully executed novel. And it presents a stronger correspondence to the "real world" of human suffering and failure. The intention was stated even before the novel was finished: ". . . It will deal with the kind of crippling of life that we have created in our society, where love is no longer the predominant feeling that we have for one another. Once love is not the feeling that dictates our social interaction with each other, then we cripple people."[13] *Tortuga* intensely dramatizes this condition. The novel is set in a children's hospital, and it relentlessly and graphically describes horrible diseases, amputations, and the nerve-shattering cries of pain and despair. Appropriately, it also extensively explores the battered psyches of society's "throw-away children." By far, it is Anaya's most sober work and it discloses a compelling tragic sense. Whereas the tragic sense was often weakened by obtrusive sentimentality in the earlier novels, in *Tortuga* it is sustained and rivets a truth about the unconscionable disposal of human beings. This is not to suggest that the tragic sense overwhelms the novel and renders it a dark and pessimistic work. To be clarified later, Anaya's mythopoesis and his faith in the regenerative power of love deny victory to the forces of death. Rather, it is meant to emphasize Anaya's large compassion for human suffering and to credit his moral vision—which refuses to tolerate the absence of love and humaneness in the world.

Mythopoesis—myth and the art of myth-making—is the crux of Anaya's philosophical and artistic vision. Precisely, Anaya's archetypal imagination is rooted in an archaism that reveres the wisdom of the past and sees this ancient wisdom as a means toward the spiritual fulfillment of humanity. It is also informed by the conviction that myth is an eternal

13. Ibid., 84.

reservoir that nourishes the most creative and the most universal art. Anaya's aesthetic credo is in accord with Northrop Frye's distinction that "myth is a form of verbal art, and belongs to the world of art. Unlike science, it deals, not with the world that man contemplates, but with the world that man creates."[14] Anaya, well-versed in mythic literature and the theory of archetypes, has repeatedly defended the validity of myth and archetypes:

> One way I have of looking at my own work . . . is through a sense that I have about primal images, primal imageries. A sense that I have about the archetypal, about what we once must have known collectively. What we all share is a kind of collective memory. . . . It simply says that there was more harmony, there was more a sense that we knew we are dust. That we had been created from it, that we were in touch with it, that we danced on it, and the dust swirled around us, and it grew the very kind of basic stuff that we need to exist. That's what I'm after. My relationship to it.[15]

Anaya's comment, of course, echoes Jung's "collective unconscious," and there are striking similarities to Jung's thoughts in *Modern Man In Search of a Soul:*

> . . . there is a thinking in primordial images—in symbols which are older than historical man; which have been ingrained in him

14. Northrop Frye, "Myth, Fiction and Displacement," *Myth and Myth Making,* ed. Henry A. Murry (New York: George Braziller, 1960), p. 164.

15. "Myth and the Writer: A Conversation with Rudolfo Anaya," 79.

from earliest times, and, eternally living, outlasting all genera-
tions, still make up the groundwork of the human psyche. It is
only possible to live the fullest life when we are in harmony with
these symbols; wisdom is a return to them.[16]

Similarly, Anaya shares with Jung, Mircea Eliade, and other
contemporary exponents of mythopoetics a concern for the
demythicization of human consciousness and the fragmenta-
tion of the human psyche. Anaya gives emphasis to terms like
polarity, duality, and *dichotomy* in describing the spiritual
and psychic debility which he sees as characteristic of
modern existence:

What did archaic men do that we cannot do? Archaic man could
communicate with both worlds. Where does dualism and polarity
come from? We can say it comes from social reality and the dia-
lectic. I disagree. I say it comes from our spiritual self, a dis-
harmonizing force. Our civilizing and socializing influence has
made us not as unified, not as harmonious, as archaic man. To
go back and get in touch, and to become more harmonious, we
go back to the unconscious and we bring out all of the symbols
and archetypals that are available to all people.[17]

Anaya's conviction that harmony and the reconciliation
of elemental forces are needed for spiritual fulfillment leads
to the holistic philosophy that forms the thematic core of

16. C. G. Jung, *Modern Man in Search of a Soul,* trans. W. S.
Dell and Cary F. Baynes (New York: Harcourt, Brace & Co., 1947),
pp. 129–30.
17. "Mitólogos y Mitómanos," 12.

his three novels. His trio of seers—Ultima in *Bless Me, Ultima,* Crispín in *Heart of Aztlán,* and Salomón in *Tortuga* —are agents of reconciliation and harmony. The oneness of things is repeatedly stated in multiple images and thematic motifs. In *Bless Me, Ultima,* a parable of good and evil in which discordant elements create dissension and violence, harmony is the greatest good. It is noteworthy that Anaya, through mythopoesis, encompasses the particular and the universal. In Antonio, the narrator and central character of the novel, Anaya projects the immemorial struggle for identity and self-knowledge. Antonio endures the rite of passage that takes him from childhood to adolescence, from innocence to incipient knowledge, and into the complex world of human affairs. His passage leads him to experience *la tristeza de la vida,* the truism that human existence is often a sad and tragic enterprise. The spiritual source that enables Antonio to overcome the disllusionment and the tragedies of life is Ultima. She brings to Antonio a holistic creed and the ultimate truth (the pun on *última,* the last and the ultimate of things, is charming and unobtrusive) that the greatest wisdom resides in the human heart. In a dream sequence, Ultima whispers to Antonio the direction that he must take toward true knowledge: "You have been seeing only parts, she finished, and not looking beyond into the great cycle that binds all." (112) Through Ultima's teachings and example, Antonio finds the moral and spiritual strength to reconcile the familial differences, the religious contraries, and the other polarities that serve as the novel's thematic conflict. The dichotomies are unified and the narrative converges in ringing affirmation: ". . . I made strength from everything that had happened to me, so that in the end even the final tragedy could not defeat me. And that is what Ultima tried to teach me, that the tragic consequences of life can be overcome by the magical strength that resides in the human heart." (237) The novel ends with a celebration of love—the unifying principle of human existence.

The conclusion of *Bless Me, Ultima* is unabashedly sentimental, and introduces an ethical prescription that is reiterated and intensified in *Heart of Aztlán* and *Tortuga*. Starting with the novel's title, *Heart of Aztlán* works the same thematic metaphor to describe the inner force that will lead to the discovery of an ancient and profound truth. The quest for *Aztlán* is, in effect, a search for the peace and harmony that have been lost throughout history and that loss has removed Chicano people from their identity and purpose. The pristine truth is that the Chicano can *return* to Aztlán; it has always existed, but people became blind to its magical presence. In an epiphany (one of Anaya's favorite devices), Clemente, like Antonio in *Bless Me, Ultima,* discovers the mythic power of Aztlán:

> Time stood still, and in that enduring moment he felt the rhythm of the heart of Aztlán beat to the measure of his own heart. Dreams and visions became reality, and reality was but the thin substance of myth and legends. A joyful power coursed from the dark womb-heart of the earth into his soul and he cried out I AM AZTLAN! (131)

True to the holistic concept that nerves Anaya's fiction, Clemente sees his place in the cosmic scheme of things and unifies the elements that previously had created alienation and confusion. Again it leads to the recognition of the superior force of love and the rejection of hatred and violence: "The real fire of heaven is not the fire of violence, it is the fire of love!" (207) The sentimental conclusion was effective in *Bless Me, Ultima,* but in *Heart of Aztlán* it is close to being a platitude. And here is where Anaya risked critical fire in suggesting that love is the answer to the oppression and injustice suffered by Chicanos.

Laced with mythopoeic images and symbols, *Tortuga* works similar metaphysical and ethical themes. Centered on a sixteen-year-old boy nicknamed "Tortuga"—due to his crippling paralysis and the "turtle cast" which he has to wear, the novel amplifies his anguish and alienation as he bitterly turns away from life and loses faith in divine providence—and himself. The resurrecting agent is Salomón, a seer and mythic figure who discloses *the path of light* (the way to reconciling wisdom and the spiritual fulfillment of the individual). Although he is a terminally-ill patient (and dies like Ultima in a similarly poignant scene), he is an abundant reservoir of spirituality and is the force that leads Tortuga to the recognition of life's value. He instructs Tortuga to appreciate and affirm the beauty of life: ". . . life is sacred, yes, even in the middle of this wasteland and in the darkness of our wards, life is sacred. . . ." (42) Like his predecessors, Salomón embodies a holistic metaphysic and celebrates the oneness of life: ". . . we're all bound together, one great force binds us all, it's the light of the sun that binds all life, the mountain and the desert, the plains and the sea." (102) The expected truism that love is the force that binds human life is dramatically (perhaps melodramatically) announced: "That's what Salomón had said. That love was the only faith which gave meaning to our race across the beach. The path of the sun was the path of love. I needed to love!" (150) Culling tropes from Eliot and other modern poets who have metaphorically described the spiritual sterility of our times, Anaya dovetails the narrative to Tortuga's realization that Salomón had left him a legacy of regenerative mythopoesis: "We must create out of our ashes. Our own hero must be born out of this wasteland, like the phoenix bird of the desert he must rise again from the ashes of our withered bodies. . . . He must walk in the path of the sun . . . and he shall sing the songs of the sun." (160) Tortuga nobly meets the task. Like Antonio in *Bless Me, Ultima,* he becomes a singer of songs; he will become a poet that will transmit the magical wisdom inherited from Ultima, Crispín, and Salomón. And, of course, he will sing songs of love. The concluding sentences of the novel describe Tortuga's homeward bound journey. His singing voice fills the bus and streams across the majestic expanse of the New Mexico desert. And Salomón's loving encouragement reverberates across the closing page: "Sing a song of love, Tortuga! Oh yes, sing of love!"

The avenue for Anaya's accomplishment in expanding

and invigorating the Chicano novel has been myth and the mythopoeic art. Here lies the core of his novelistic invention. His archetypal imagination richly mines indigenous materials, fuses them with poetic images and symbols, and connects the past and the present to make something new from the old. On a smaller scale, Anaya possesses the gift and achieves the art credited to one of the twentieth-century exemplars of mythopoesis, Thomas Mann: "In a narrative tone that recalls the past, he reveals what we find disturbing in the present. He is at once old and new, and his gift is the mingling of the mythic and the present moment."[18]

At one point in *Tortuga,* Salomón explains the mythologizing behind his stories: "Each carries a new story, but all these stories are bound to the same theme . . . *life is sacred.*" (42) Similarly, each of Anaya's novels presents a new story, but they are bound by one central theme: life is sacred and the love of life is the greatest human accomplishment. Anaya cherishes the kinder moments of the human race and sings a song that seeks to bind humanity. There is much truth in his song, and there is a largeness of heart in the man and his work. Anaya's work is eloquent testament that art can teach us to recognize our humanity. It is an exemplary achievement.

18. Wright Morris, *About Fiction* (New York: Harper & Row, 1975), p. 145.

Works by and about
Rudolfo A. Anaya

TERESA MÁRQUEZ

TO MY KNOWLEDGE, the following bibliography on works by and about Rudolfo Anaya is the most complete of its kind. Besides the more obvious entries, such as Anaya's three novels—*Bless Me, Ultima, Heart of Aztlán,* and *Tortuga*—and the two collections of his stories—*Cuentos: Tales of the Southwest* and *Cuentos Chicanos*—it includes essays both by Anaya himself (in particular the important piece on "la tierra," or sense of place, which appeared in slightly varying forms in several publications) and by students of his work. Some of the latter pieces, originally completed as class assignments, are most valuable, in that they explore, in depth, literary questions that of necessity have been only touched upon in reviews of the author's work. I am particularly pleased to include the entry of Anaya's soon-to-be-published collection of short stories, *Silence of the Llano,* which will be brought out in the fall of 1982.

The entries in the bibliography have been arranged for the most part in alphabetical order. When a second person has cooperated with Anaya, either as coauthor or editor, the name of the collaborist has been placed second so that works even in part authored by Anaya might all be included in his name. Unsigned reviews of his works have been listed under *reviews of* the particular work in question.

I am indebted more than I can say to the research of Ernestine Eger in the Chicano Studies program at the University of California, Berkeley. I was first made aware of her wonderfully complete bibliography on Anaya through the alertness of the Ethnic Studies section of the General Library of the University of New Mexico. A more complete galley of the bibliography, with additional listings, was provided me by Francisco Garcia, head of the Chicano Studies Library at the University of California, Berkeley, which later published Ms. Eger's bibliography in *A Bibliography of Criticism of Contemporary Chicano Literature.* Again and again I was impressed by Ms. Eger's thoroughness in her project, which included not only the obvious entries, but also the more obscure.

I am grateful to Donald Farren, head of the Special Collections department of the General Library at the University of New Mexico, and to his staff, for facilitating access to the collection of pieces by and about Anaya. I am particularly indebted to their student assistant Mary Kay McCarthy, who checked details for me and provided me with her undivided attention. I must also express deep gratitude and appreciation to Nancy Gail Gilliland, without whose help I would not have been able to successfully accomplish this project. Lastly, I wish to thank the Dean of Library Services, Paul Vassallo, for asking me to compile this bibliography. It has been a great opportunity for me, and a marvelous learning experience.

BIBLIOGRAPHY

Alves Pereira, Teresinha. Review of *Bless Me, Ultima,* by Rudolfo Anaya. *Hispamerica: Revista de Literatura, No.* 4–5 (1973): 137–39.
A fairly detailed and informative review written entirely in Spanish. The novel's theme, characters, story action and culture are discussed.

Anaya, Rudolfo. "B. Traven is Alive and Well in Cuernavaca." *Escolios,* IV, Nos. 1–2 (Mayo-Noviembre 1979): 1–12.
Short story. An autobigraphical account of the author's encounter with Justino, an unforgettable character and a man of many talents.

———. *Bless Me, Ultima.* Berkeley: Quinto Sol Publications, Inc. 1972.
A narrative about a young boy's rite of passage, set in rural New Mexico. The young protagonist's initiation is guided by Ultima, a family friend and curandera. Myths, legends, customs and values evoke a rich story.

———. "Carta de Rudolfo Anaya." *Caracol,* I, No. 9 (May 1975): 4.
Copy of letter refusing publication in *Chicano Voices.*

———. "The Closing of Mack-Ellens." *Albuquerque News,* 15 February 1978, pp. 1, 4.

A short story about urban renewal. Two "comadres" discuss the effects of progress.

———. "Cuentos de los Antepasados." *Agenda: A Journal of Hispanic Issues,* 9 (January-February 1979): 11.
Copy not reviewed.

———. Excerpts from *Bless Me, Ultima. El Grito,* V, No. 3 (Spring 1972): 4–17.
A short autobiography is included.

———. Excerpts from *Bless Me, Ultima.* In *Southwest Fiction.* Ed. Max Apple. New York: Bantam Books, 1981.

———. *Heart of Aztlán.* Berkeley: Editorial Justa Publications, Inc., 1976.
Heart of Aztlán is a narrative about a family's move from their rural home to a barrio in the city. The story explores the family's struggle against oppression, cultural encroachment, and loss of values and customs.

———. "In Commemoration: One Million Volumes." *A Million Stars: The Millionth Acquisition for the University of New Mexico General Library.* Ed. Connie Capers Thorson. Albuquerque, N.M.: The University of New Mexico General Library, 1981, pp. 9–15.
An address delivered at the commemoration of the acquisition of the millionth volume at the University of New Mexico General Library. Anaya speaks of the role libraries played in his development as a writer.

———. "Mexico Mystique—Another View." *New Mexico Magazine,* 53, No. 11 (November, 1975): 37.
A review of Frank Waters' *Mexico Mystique,* a book of myths and symbols of pre-Columbian America.

———. Personal interview. 1976.

Bibliography

Rudolfo Anaya is interviewed by three faculty members at the Audio Visual Center, El Paso Community College in El Paso, Texas. *"Bless Me, Ultima:* A Novel," video recording. Cassette, 37 mins.

———. "The Place of the Swallows." In *Voices from the Rio Grande: Selections from the First Rio Grande Writers Conference.* Albuquerque, N.M.: A Rio Grande Writers Association Press Book, 1976, pp. 98-106.

Short story about a group of boys, members of a tribe, on an exploration trip into unknown territory. The protagonist chooses to leave the tribe after the leader commands them to kill the swallows on the cliffs. Deals with myths, self-identification, aloneness, and the temptation of the human being to turn to primitive behavior when in the wilds.

———. "Requiem for a Lowrider." *La Confluencia: A Magazine of the Southwest,* 2, No. 2-3 (October 1978): 2-6. A commencement address to the Albuquerque High School Class of 1978.

Excerpt from address appeared in the *Albuquerque News* (28 June 1978), Sec. A, pp. A1, A7.

———. *Silence of the Llano.* To be published.

A collection of short stories. Some are hilariously entertaining.

———. "Southwest Christmas: A Mosaic of Rituals Celebrates Spiritual, Community Renewal." *Los Angeles Times,* 27 December 1981, Sec. IV, p. 3, col. 1.

A warm narration of Christmas celebrations in New Mexico.

———. *Tortuga.* Berkeley: Editorial Justa Publications, Inc.,

1979.

A narrative about a young man crippled in an accident. Set in a children's hospital, the story explores human suffering, love, death and courage. *Tortuga* is the last of Anaya's New Mexico trilogy.

———. "A Writer Discusses His Craft." *The CEA Critic: An Official Journal of the College English Association,* Vol. XL, No. 1 (November 1977): 39–43.

A limited discussion of the writer's sense of "landscape" or "la tierra" in the creative process.

———. "The Writer's Inscape." Abstract. *Rocky Mountain Review of Language and Literature,* 30, No. 3 (Summer 1976): 161–62.

An abstract of Anaya's paper presented before a symposium on Ethnic Studies.

———. "The Writer's Landscape: Epiphany in Landscape." *Latin American Literary Review,* V, No. 10 (Spring-Summer 1977): 98-102.

A limited discussion of Anaya's "sense of place" or "la tierra."

———. "The Writer's Landscape: Epiphany in Landscape." In *Southwest: A Contemporary Anthology.* Ed. Karl and Jane Kopp. Albuquerque, N.M.: Red Earth Press, 1977, pp. 175–79.

———. "The Writer's Sense of Place: A Symposium and Commentaries," ed. John R. Milton. *South Dakota Review,* 13, No. 3 (Autumn 1975): 66–67.

A symposium on regionalism. Anaya expresses his views on the subject of "sense of place."

———. "The Writer's Viewpoint: Reaction to María Hoffman's Paper." MLA Conference, New York. December 1978.

Copy not available for review.

———. and Antonio Márquez. *Cuentos Chicanos*. Albuquerque, N.M.: Department of American Studies, The University of New Mexico, 1980.

A collection of short stories by writers from the Southwest. These stories, written in English and Spanish, represent a variety of style and content.

"Anaya Speaks on Job of Artist." *New Mexico Summer Lobo,* 21 June 1974, p. 3.

This article is on Anaya's lecture "Conversation with Ultima," presented through the Lecture Under the Stars series on the UNM campus.

"Anaya Wins $10,000 Chicano Writing Award." *Coda: Poets & Writers Newsletter,* 6, No. 3 (February-March 1979): 15.

Announcement of Anaya's National Chicano Council on Higher Education fellowship.

Armas, José. "Chicano Writing: The New Mexico Narrative." *De Colores,* 5, No. 1–2 (1980): 69-81.

A brief overview of Chicano literature in New Mexico. Rudolfo Anaya's *Bless Me, Ultima* and *Heart of Aztlán* are discussed briefly and cited as examples of "the collective unconscious of the cultural traditions of the past with the present."

"Barrio Life in Albuquerque." Review of *Heart of Aztlán* by Rudolfo Anaya. *Albuquerque Journal,* 13 February 1977, Sec. D, p. 3.

A very short discussion of plot and theme.

Bilingualism: Promise for Tomorrow. Pasadena: Bilingual Educational Services, 1977.

Rudolfo Anaya wrote a 10-minute script on bilingual education for this 16 mm., 30-minute color film.

Black, Charlotte. "Rudolfo Anaya—Fulfilling A Heritage." *Albuquerque Tribune,* 10 December 1979, Accent section.

An interview with Anaya about his writing activities, including the publication of *Tortuga,* his third novel.

Blanco, Manuel. "Reseñas: An Outstanding Collection." Review of *Cuentos: Tales from the Hispanic Southwest* by José Griego y Maestas and Rudolfo Anaya. *Revista Rio Bravo,* 1, No. 2 (1981): 12, 19.

A review of tales written in English and Spanish. The stories were collected originally by Juan B. Rael.

Brito, Aristeo, Jr. "Paraíso, Caída Y Regeneración en Tres Novelas Chicanas." *DAI,* 39 (1978): 2268-A (The University of Arizona).

A plot synopsis of Brito's study of the "paradise-fall-regeneration" pattern in *Pocho, Bless Me, Ultima* and *Peregrinos De Aztlán. Bless Me, Ultima* offers the broader view of the three-stage pattern. Moreover, the novel is an affirmation of the Hispanic culture in New Mexico.

Bruce-Novoa. *Chicano Authors: Inquiry by Interview,* Austin: University of Texas Press, 1980.

Rudolfo Anaya is one of several Chicano writers interviewed. Anaya responds to questions about personal background and Chicano literature.

———. "Portraits of the Chicano Artist as a Young Man: The

Bibliography

Making of the 'Author' in Three Chicano Novels."
Festival Floricanto II. Albuquerque, New Mexico:
Pajarito Publishers, 1977, pp. 150–61.

A brief but scholarly treatment of the concept of literary space and the "interior author" in three novels including *Bless Me, Ultima.*

———. Review of *Heart of Aztlán. La Confluencia*, I, Nos. 3–4
(July 1977): 61–62.

Brief critical review.

———. "The Space of Chicano Literature." *De Colores,* 1,
No. 4 (1975): 22–41.

A profound and scholarly analysis of "literary space" in Chicano literature. *Bless Me, Ultima* is one of several Chicano works included in this study to illustrate how "literary space" functions. Reprinted in *The Chicano Literary World—1974.* Proceedings of The First National Symposium on Chicano Literature and Critical Analysis.

Bucco, Martin. Review of *Bless Me, Ultima,* by Rudolfo
Anaya. *Southwestern American Literature,* 2, No. 3
(Winter 1972): 153–54.

In a brief but critical review, Anaya's "spiritual autobiography," *Bless Me, Ultima* is described as a "pastoral elegy."

Burstein, Daniel. "A Proud Society Fights for its Life."
Macleans, 95, No. 11 (15 March 1982): 12, 17–18, 20.
Rudolfo Anaya is one of several New Mexicans quoted in this article on the problems faced by the Hispanic and Indian communities as a result of New Mexico's growth and change.

63

Candelaria, Cordelia. "Anahuac Again and Chicano Writers." Review of *The Luck of Huemac* by Daniel Peters. *American Book Review,* 4, No. 1 (January-February 1982).

Copy not reviewed. Article alludes to Rudolfo Anaya.

———. "Los Ancianos in Chicano Literature." *Agenda, IX,* No. 6 (November-December 1979). 19–21.

Copy not available for review. Article alludes to Rudolfo Anaya.

———. "On Rudolfo Anaya." *Encyclopedia of Chicano Literature.* Ed. Julio A. Martinez. Greenwood Press (forthcoming).

This encyclopedia will include a 25-page biocritical article on Rudolfo Anaya.

Cantu, Roberto. "Degradación y Regeneración en *Bless Me, Ultima:* El Chicano y la Vida Nueva." *The Identification and Analysis of Chicano Literature.* Ed. Francisco Jimenez. New York: Bilingual Press/Editorial Bilingüe, 1979, pp. 374–87.

A scholarly study, in Spanish, of specific elements and "un sentido subyacente" present in *Bless Me, Ultima.*

———. "Estructura y Sentido de lo Onírico en *Bless Me, Ultima. Mester,* V, No. 1 (Noviembre 1974): 27–41.

This detailed analysis of the dream sequences in *Bless Me, Ultima* is written entirely in Spanish. The dreams, classified into three categories: conflict and reconciliation; destiny and transformation; and prophecy and revelation, are examined according to their thematic significance, their relation to the plot, and their meaning in the novel.

———. "Estructura y Sentido de lo Onírico en *Bless Me, Ultima*." Trans. Barbara L. Wiard. University of New Mexico, 1977.

This is an unofficial and unpublished English translation submitted as a class project.

———. Review of *Bless Me, Ultima by* Rudolfo A. Anaya. *Mester,* IV, No. 1 (Noviembre 1973): 66–68.

Plot synopsis and interpretative review. Written in Spanish.

Cárdenas Dwyer, Carlota. "Chicano Literature 1965–1975: The Flowering of the Southwest." Ph.D. diss., State University of New York at Stony Brook, 1976.

An examination of the major genres of modern Chicano literature: drama, poetry, and the novel. A whole chapter is devoted to an interpretation of *Bless Me, Ultima.*

———. "Myth and Folk Culture in Contemporary Chicano Literature." *La Luz* (December 1974): 28–29.

A limited discussion of the character Ultima and "curanderismo" in *Bless Me, Ultima.*

Carrillo, Loretta. "The Search for Selfhood and Order in Contemporary Chicano Fiction." *DAI,* 40 (1980): 4034-A (Michigan State University).

This study illustrates the struggle for self-identification suggested in seven Chicano novels. *Bless Me, Ultima* and *Heart of Aztlán* are included as representative of the rural and urban experiences.

Castro, Donald F. "Chicano Literature: A Bibliographical Essay." *English in Texas,* 7, No. 4. (Summer 1976): 14–19.

Developed as a teaching module for the Teacher Center

Program at the University of Texas at El Paso, this essay discusses briefly the selections included in the bibliography provided. *Bless Me, Ultima* is one of the works recommended.

Chávez, Fray Angelico. Review of *Bless Me, Ultima* by Rudolfo A. Anaya. *New Mexico Magazine,* 50, No. 3–4 (March-April 1973): 46.

A short critical review.

———. Review of *Heart of Aztlán* by Rudolfo A. Anaya. *New Mexico Magazine,* 55, No. 6 (June 1977): 36.

A brief favorable review.

Cheuse, Alan. "The Voice of the Chicano: Letter from the Southwest." *New York Times Book Review,* 11 October 1981, pp. 15, 36–37.

A brief analysis of the literary activity in the Southwestern United States. The article concentrates on Rudolfo Anaya and his works, *Bless Me, Ultima* and *Cuentos, Tales from the Hispanic Southwest.*

"Chicano Literary Award Winner Among Speakers." *The New Mexican,* 5 May 1974, Sec. A, p. 9.

Press release on Rudolfo Anaya's talk for the Book and Author luncheon for the benefit of St. John's College Library.

Chicano Scholars and Writers: A Bio-Bibliographical Directory. Ed. Julio A. Martinez. Metuchen, N.J.: The Scarecrow Press, Inc., 1979, pp. 22–23.

Entry for Rudolfo Anaya includes a short bibliography for 1972-77.

Curran, Colleen. "Author Receives Writing Grant." *UNM Daily Lobo,* 12 September 1978, p. 8.

Bibliography

Press release on Rudolfo Anaya's National Chicano Council on Higher Education $10,000 grant.

Cinquemani, Frank. Review of *Bless Me, Ultima* by Rudolfo A. Anaya. *Library Journal,* 98, No. 3 (1 February 1973): 433.
A very short favorable review.

Cohen, Saul. "The 10 Best Novels of New Mexico." *New Mexico Magazine,* 52, No. 3–4 (March-April 1974): 22–23, 26–27.
Bless Me, Ultima is one of several novels recommended for tenth place.

Contemporary Authors: Bio-Bibliographical Guide to Current Authors and Their Works. Ed. Clare D. Kinsman. Detroit: Gale Research Co., 1974, p. 19.
Entry for Rudolfo Anaya includes information on personal background, career, writings, and sidelines.

Davila, Luis. Review of *Bless Me, Ultima,* by Rudolfo A. Anaya. *Revista Chicano-Riqueña,* 1, No. 2 (Fall 1973): 53–54.
A brief plot synopsis and favorable review.

De la Garza, Rudolf O. and Rowena Rivera. "The Socio-Political World of the Chicano: A Comparative Analysis of Social Scientific and Literary Perspectives." *Minority Language and Literature: Retrospective and Perspective.* Ed. Dexter Fisher. New York: Modern Language Association of America, 1977, pp. 42–64.
Bless Me, Ultima is one of three novels selected for this study because it is considered representative of the second stage of development of Chicano literature.

Donnelly, Dyan. "Finding a Home in the Wall." Review of

Bless Me, Ultima by Rudolfo Anaya. *The Bilingual Review/La Revista Bilingüe,* 1, No. 1 (January-April 1974): 113–18.

A plot synopsis and critical review of novel's strengths and weaknesses.

Eger, Ernestina. *A Bibliography of Criticism of Contemporary Chicano Literature.* Berkeley: Chicano Studies Library, University of California, 1981.

This bibliography contains an exhaustive list on Rudolfo Anaya.

Gallegos, Mary Louise. "Rudolfo A. Anaya: Local Author Achieves Success." *Model Cities News,* 15 September 1975, p. 1.

A bilingual interview. Brief, concentrates on Anaya's personal background.

García, Mario Trinidad. "Chicano Writers and Chicanismo." Review of *Bless Me, Ultima* by Rudolfo A. Anaya. *La Luz,* 4, No. 2 (May 1975): 43.

Brief critical review.

Gard, Wayne. Review of *Bless Me, Ultima* by Rudolfo A. Anaya. *Southwest Review,* LVIII, No. 2 (Spring 1973): vii.

A very brief commentary on plot and themes.

Garzón, Luz Elena. "La Cuesta Religiosa." Seminario de Literatura Chicana. University of California, San Diego, 1974.

Paper on *Bless Me, Ultima* for Juan Rodriguez, director. Copy not available for review.

"Gente." *Nuestro,* 2, No. 11 (November 1978): 62.

Announcement of Rudolfo Anaya's award from Na-

Bibliography

tional Council for Higher Education.

Gerdes, Dick. Review of *Cuentos Chicanos* by Rudolfo Anaya and Antonio Márquez. *Hispania* 64 (December 1981): 642–43.

This review discusses the contents of the collection, writing styles, themes, and the writers.

Gish, Robert F. "Curanderismo and Witchery in the Fiction of Rudolfo A. Anaya: The Novel as Magic." *New Mexico Humanities Review*, 2, No. 2 (Summer 1979): 5–12.

A thought-provoking exploration of the "sense of the heroine" in *Bless Me, Ultima* and *Heart of Aztlán*.

Griego y Maestas, José and Rudolfo A. Anaya. *Cuentos: Tales From the Hispanic Southwest*. Santa Fe: The Museum of New Mexico Press, 1980.

The tales or cuentos in this collection are based on stories collected by Juan B. Rael. The stories are in English and Spanish.

Haddox, John. Review of "Heart of Aztlán." *Sundial*, 15 May 1977, p. 20.

Copy not available for review.

Hinojosa, Rolando. "Mexican-American Literature: Toward an Identification." *Books Abroad*, 49, No. 3–4 (1975): 422–30.

A paper on the nature and place of Mexican-American literature in American literature. *Bless Me, Ultima* is described as a "strictly Mexican-American novel, bearing a resemblance to the modern American novel."

Hoffman, María López. "Myth and Reality in Heart of Aztlán." MLA Conference, New York. December 1978.

Copy of paper not available for review.

Janowski, Jack. "22 Offerings in 'Cuentos'." *Albuquerque Journal,* 22 June 1980, Sec. D, p. 8.

A brief description of *Cuentos Chicanos,* a collection of twenty-two short stories in English and Spanish edited by Rudolfo Anaya.

———. "State's Writers in '77 Produced Wealth, Variety, Interest." *Albuquerque Journal,* 25 December 1977, Sec. E, p. 2.

This article on New Mexico's writers highlights Albuquerque authors including Rudolfo Anaya.

———. " 'Tortgua' Novel Completes Rudolfo Anaya's Trilogy." *Albuquerque Journal,* 4 November 1979, Sec. D, p. 3.

An interview and brief review.

———. "New Novel Vividly Shows Albuquerque Barrio Life." *Albuquerque Journal,* 27 February 1977, Sec. D, p. 3.

A favorable book review of Anaya's second novel, *Heart of Aztlán.*

Johnson, David. Review of *Heart of Aztlán,* by Rudolfo Anaya. *Puerto del Sol,* 16 (Spring 1981): 121–23.

A plot synopsis and mildly critical review of Anaya's second novel.

———. and David Apodaca. "Myth and the Writer: A Conversation With Rudolfo Anaya." *New America,* 3, No. 3 (Spring 1979); 76–85.

In this interview Johnson and Apodaca ask a wide-ranging series of questions, beginning with Anaya's personal background. Although Anaya is open in expressing his thoughts on religion, the Chicano literary movement, self-actualization and the literary landscape, he does not discuss Ultima.

Johnson, Elaine Dorough. "A Thematic Study of Three Chicano Narratives: *Estampas Del Valle Y Otras Obras, Bless Me, Ultima* and *Peregrinos De Aztlán.* DAI, 39 (1978): 3614-A (The University of Wisconsin, Madison).

Two major themes are identified and analyzed: cultural and historial, and social, political and economic.

Johnson, Richard. "Rudolfo A. Anaya: A Vision of the Heroic." *Empire Magazine,* 2 March 1980, pp. 25, 29.

An interview. A discussion of Anaya's creative achievements, specifically *Bless Me, Ultima.*

Kopp, Karl. Review of *Heart of Aztlán* by Rudolfo A. Anaya. *Pawn Review* 2, No. 2 (Winter 1977): 80–83.

Copy not available for review.

———. "Two Views on *Heart of Aztlán.*" Review of *Heart of Aztlán. La Confluencia,* 1, No. 3–4 (July 1977): 62–63.

A thoughtful and generally positive review.

Knudson, Cynthia. "La Llorona Still Lives." *Multi-Ethnicity in American Publishing,* 6, No. 3 (Fall 1978): 5–6.

Copy not available for review.

Laird, W. David. Review of *Heart of Aztlán* by Rudolfo A. Anaya. *Books of the Southwest,* No. 228 (November 1977): 1.

Copy not available.

Lattin, Vernon E. "Ethnicity and Identity in the Contemporary Novel." *Minority Voices,* 2, No. 2 (Fall 1978): 37–44.

This essay explores the Chicano protagonist's struggle with self-identification and ethnicity. *Bless Me, Ultima* is one of several autobiographical novels examined.

———. "The Horror of Darkness: Meaning and Structure in Anaya's *Bless Me, Ultima." Revista Chicano-Riqueña,* VI, No. 2 (Spring 1978): 51-57.

An analysis of the death scenes, dream sequences, and the protagonist's experience with the "horror of darkness."

———. "The Quest for Mythic Vision in Contemporary Native American and Chicano Fiction." *American Literature,* 50, No. 4 (January 1979): 625–40.

Bless Me, Ultima is analyzed as a religious novel expressing the rejection of Christianity and the embracing of paganism in the process of achieving the sacred vision.

Leal, Luis, et al. *A Decade of Chicano Literature (1970-1979): Critical Essays and Bibliography.* Santa Barbara, Ca.: Editorial La Causa, 1982.

The bibliography contains a number of entries on Rudolfo Anaya.

———. "The Problem of Identifying Chicano Literature." *The Identification and Analysis of Chicano Literature.* Ed. Francisco Jimenez. New York: Bilingual Press/ Editorial Bilingüe, 1979, pp. 2–6.

Bless Me, Ultima is cited as an example of the novel

using myth and legends to express the universal through the regional.

Lomelí, Francisco A. and Donald W. Urioste. Review of *Bless Me, Ultima* and *Heart of Aztlán. Chicano Perspectives in Literature.* Albuquerque, NM.: Pajarito Publications, 1976, pp. 39–40.

Brief discussions of basic themes. Clear and concise reviews.

———. and Donald W. Urioste. Review of *Heart of Aztlán. De Colores,* 3, No. 4 (1977): 81–82.

A succinct review of *Heart of Aztlán.*

Mitchell, Carol. "Rudolfo Anaya's *Bless Me, Ultima:* Folk Culture in Literature." *Critique* XXII, No. 1 (1980): 55–64.

This is a study of traditional rural Hispanic culture, specifically the family, role expectations for men and women, and the natural conflict between male and female values, the close ties between the natural and supernatural world, and curanderismo and brujería. Ultima's role as a curandera and her magical practices are discussed.

"Mitólogos y Mitómanos: Mesa Redonda con Alurista, R. Anaya, M. Herrera Sobeck, A. Morales y H. Viramontes." *Maize: Notebooks of Xicano Art and Literature,* 4, No. 3–4 (Spring-Summer 1981): 6–23.

Discussion on the definition of the myth of Aztlán, definition of myth in Chicano literature, and function and use of myth in Chicano literature.

Moody, Michael, "Platica con Rudy Anaya." *Caracol,* 1

(March 1975): 3–4.
  Anaya talks about his sense of stories, including *Bless Me, Ultima* and Chicano literature.

Newman, Katherine. "An Ethnic Literary Scholar Views American Literature." *Melus,* 7 No. 1 (1980): 3–19.
  This paper on the ethnic approach to American literature devotes a segment to *Bless Me, Ultima,* identified as an "eccentric" ethnic work.

"NM Author Speaks at GI Forum Meet." *The New Mexican,* 16 June 1974, Sec. A, p. 3. Reprint. *Comexaz News Monitoring Service,* June 1974, p. 243.
  Article on Rudolfo Anaya's talk on the organization's activities in promoting the self-help concept.

Nordstrand, Dave. "$4 Million TV Film for NM." *Albuquerque Tribune,* 1 August, 1980, Sec. A, p. 11.
  This article reports plans for a made-for-TV movie, based on *Bless Me, Ultima,* to be filmed in New Mexico.

Ortiz Pinchetti, Francisco. "La Cultura Chicana, Amenazada por la Brutalidad Anglosajona: Rudolfo Anaya." *Proceso: Seminario de Información y Analisis,* 6, No. 263 (16 November 1981): 46–47.
  First part of interview focuses on the Bloomfield incident in which copies of *Bless Me, Ultima* were burned. Second half concentrates on the novel and Anaya's personal background.

Pacheco, Javier. Review of *Heart of Aztlán. Rayas.* No. 1 January-February 1978): 10–11.
  Copy not available.

Paredes, Raymond A. "The Evolution of Chicano Liter-

Bibliography

ature." *Melus,* 5, No. 2 (Spring 1978): 71–110.

An exhaustive study of the development of and influences in Chicano literature. Rudolfo Anaya is cited as a Chicano novelist who, although writing in the Anglo-American literary style, stills retains his ethnic distinctiveness.

———. "The Promise of Chicano Literature." *Minority Language and Literature: Retrospective and Perspective.* Ed. Dexter Fisher. New York: Modern Languages Association of America, 1977, pp. 29–41.

An essay on the literary distinctiveness of Chicano literature in American literature. *Bless Me, Ultima,* one of the novels analyzed, reflects a vigorous and thriving literature.

Paul Phillips, Aileen, "Collection of Chicano Short Stories; Good Reading." Review of *Cuentos Chicanos* by Rudolfo Anaya and Antonio Márquez. *The New Mexican,* 20 November 1980, Sec. D. p. 8.

A descriptive review of the collection.

Pino, Frank, Jr. "The Outsider and 'El Otro' in Tomás Rivera's ' . . . Y No Se Lo Tragó La Tierra'." *Books Abroad,* 49, No. 3 (Summer 1975): 453–58.

In this essay *Bless Me, Ultima* is briefly mentioned as an example of "conflicting values within the immediate family setting."

Portillo-Orozco, Febe. "Rudolfo Anaya's Use of History, Myth and Legend in His Novels: *Bless Me, Ultima* and *Heart of Aztlán.*" M.A. thesis, San Francisco State University, 1981.

A study of the use of legends, myths, history, and religion of Meso-american people in Anaya's novels. Also examined are uses of symbolic characterizations and archetypes.

Ray J. Karen. "Cultural and Mythical Archetypes in Rudolfo Anaya's *Bless Me, Ultima*." *New Mexico Humanities Review*, 1, No. 3 (September 1978): 23–28. A study of Antonio, the young protagonist, as an archetypal representation of the contemporary Chicano.

Reed, Ishmael. "An Interview With Rudolfo Anaya." *San Francisco Review of Books*, 4, No. 2 (June 1978): 9–12, 34. Copy not available for review.

Review of *Heart of Aztlán* by Rudolfo A. Anaya. *Los Desarraigados*, 4, No. 5 (Winter 1976–77): 16. Copy not available for review.

Review of *Heart of Aztlán* by Rudolfo A. Anaya. *Multi-Ethnicity in American Publishing*, 6, No. 3 (Fall 1978): 2. Copy not available for review.

Rodrígues, Raymond J. *"Bless Me, Ultima* by Rudolfo A. Anaya." In "A Novel (Poem, Story, Essay) to teach." Comp. Susan Koch. *English Journal*, 65, No. 1 (January 1976): 63–64. Copy not available for review.

Rodríguez, José. Dir. *The Season of La Llorona*. By Rudolfo Anaya. Kimo Theatre, Albuquerque, New Mexico, 21–23 December 1979. A three-act play about legends, myths, and the conquest of Mexico.

Rodríguez, Juan. "La Búsqueda de Identidad y Sus Motivos

en la Literatura Chicana." *The Identification and Analysis of Chicano Literature*. Ed. Francisco Jimenez. New York: Bilingual Press/Editorial Bilingüe, 1979, pp. 170–78.

A discussion on the search for self-identification. *Bless Me, Ultima* is one of the novels mentioned in the study.

———. Review of *Heart of Aztlán*. *Carta Abierta*, No. 7 (February 1977): 3–4.

A very brief commentary on *Heart of Aztlán*.

Rodríguez del Pino, Salvador. *Interview With Rudolfo Anaya*. Encuentro With Chicano Writers Series. Santa Barbara: Center for Chicano Studies. University of California, 1977.

Interview video recorded. Cassette. 30 minutes. Copy not available for review.

Rogers, Jane. "The Function of the La Llorona Motif in Rudolfo Anaya's *Bless Me, Ultima*." *Latin American Literary Review*, V, No. 10 (Spring-Summer 1977): 64–69.

A comparison of la llorona to the Sirens in *The Odyssey*. Examines the development of the theme as a literal myth and as an integral part of the protagonist's life.

———. Review of *Heart of Aztlán*. *Latin American Literary Review*, V, No. 10 (Spring-Summer 1977): 143–45.

A concise analytical review. Brief comparison between *Heart of Aztlán* and *Bless Me Ultima*.

Salazar Parr, Carmen. "Current Trends in Chicano Literary Criticism." *The Identification and Analysis of Chicano Literature*. Ed. Francisco Jimenez. New York: Bilingual Press/Editorial Bilingüe, 1979, pp. 134–42.

Summary of recent critical works. An in-depth study of *Bless Me, Ultima* is discussed briefly.

Salmón, Roberto M. Review of *Cuentos Chicanos*. *New Mexico Historical Review,* 56, No. 1 (1981): 111–12. A comparison between *Cuentos* and *American Indian Poetry*.

Segade, Gustavo V. "Una Panorama Conceptual de la Novela Chicana." *Fomento Literario,* No. 3 (invierno 1973): 5–17.
An analysis of *Bless Me, Ultima* and three other Chicano novels. Explores four main themes: self-identification, oppression, culture, and Chicano history.

Sommers, Joseph. "Critical Approaches to Chicano Literature." *The Identification and Analysis of Chicano Literature*. Ed. Francisco Jimenez. New York: Bilingual Press/Editorial Bilingüe, 1979, pp. 143–52.
Bless Me, Ultima is referred to as a novel expressing distinctive cultural elements.

Somoza, Oscar U. "Hacia una Nueva Visión Espiritual en *Bless Me, Ultima.*" Unpublished paper. Not available for review.

–––. "Visión Axiologica en la Narrativa Chicana." *DAI,* 38 (1978); 4203-A (The University of Arizona, 1977). Survey of the Chicano value system and world view in nine Chicano novels including *Bless Me, Ultima*.

Tatum, Charles. *A Selected and Annotated Bibliography of Chicano Studies*. 2nd ed. 1979. Lincoln, Neb.: Society of Spanish and Spanish-American Studies.
This bibliography contains a number of entries on Rudolfo Anaya.

Bibliography

Testa, Daniel. "Extensive/Intensive Dimensionality in Anaya's *Bless Me, Ultima.*" *Latin American Literary Review,* V, No. 10 (Spring-Summer 1977): 70–78.

Exhaustive examination of the various elements in *Bless Me, Ultima*: dramatic action, narrative intensification, time element, stereotypes, and others.

Todd Hooper, Glenda. Review of *Bless Me, Ultima. The Booklist,* 72, No. 8 (15 December 1975): 557.

A one sentence statement on the novel.

Tonn, Horst. "Themen und Erzähltechniken der Chicano Literatur: Rudolfo A. Anaya, *Bless Me, Ultima,* Tomás Rivera, . . . *Y no se lo Tragó la Tierra.*" Ph.D. diss. Free University of Berlin, 1981.

Tonn identifies some basic themes found in Chicano literature: search for individual and collective identity, religion, social criticism, and protest. Their occurrence in *Bless Me, Ultima* is discussed.

Trejo, Arnulfo. Review of *Bless Me, Ultima. Arizona Quarterly,* 29, No. 1 (Spring 1973): 95–96.

Plot synopsis; favorable review.

Treviño, Albert D. "Bless Me, Ultima: A Critical Interpretation." *De Colores,* 3, No. 4 (1977): 30–33.

A pithy interpretation from four viewpoints: "that of the realist, the moralist, the expressionist, and the structuralist."

Treviño, Oscar. "Manipulation of Power in *Heart of Aztlán.*" Unpublished paper.

Not available.

———. "Tension and Resolution in *Bless Me, Ultima.*" Unpublished paper.

Not available.

Turner, Alice. Review of *Bless Me, Ultima*. *Publisher's Weekly*, 204, No. 11 (18 March 1974): 54.

One paragraph review.

Unpingco-Garrett, Regina. "Images of Women in *Bless Me, Ultima*." *Visión* (Spring 1976): 41–42.

Not available for review.

Urioste, Donaldo. "Literary Scope of the Rites of Passage in *Bless Me, Ultima*." The Pacific Coast Council on Latin American Studies 26th Annual Conference, Laguna Beach, October 1980.

An analysis of the young protagonist's maturation process and loss of innocence.

Valdés, Ricardo. "Defining Chicano Literature or the Perimeter of Literary Space." *Latin American Literary Review*, V, No. 10 (Spring-Summer 1977): 16–22.

An essay on the definition of Chicano literature; literary space in Chicano literature and critical approaches to Chicano literature. References to *Bless Me, Ultima* are included.

Valdés Fallis, Guadalupe. "Metaphysical Anxiety and the Existence of God in Contemporary Chicano Fiction." *Revista Chicano-Riqueña*, 3, No. 1 (Winter 1975): 26–33.

This study attempts to dispel doubts about the validity of Chicano fiction as expression of "mainstream contemporary thought and culture." *Bless Me, Ultima* is discussed as an example of a universal novel.

Waggoner, Amy. "Tony's Dreams—An Important Dimension in *Bless Me, Ultima*." *Southwestern American*

Literature, IV (1974): 74–79.

A succinct analysis of the dream sequences as reflections of the major themes in the novel.

Wilson, Carter. "Magical Strength in the Human Heart." Review of *Bless Me, Ultima. Ploughshares,* 4, No. 3 (June 1978): 190–97.

Plot synopsis and critical review.

Wood, Scott. Review of *Bless Me, Ultima. America,* 128, No. 3 (27 June 1973): 72–74.

Plot synopsis and limited discussion of themes.

Woods, Richard D. "The Chicano Novel: Silence After Publications." *Revista Chicano-Riqueña,* 4, No. 3 (Summer 1976): 42–47.

A survey of the number of reviews accorded each of six Chicano novels, including *Bless Me, Ultima,* in mainstream trade journals and book review publications.

A Note on the Illustrations

DONALD FARREN

THE ILLUSTRATIONS APPEARING in this book lend a sympathetic visual representation to themes evoked in Rudolfo Anaya's essay. They are based on prints made by Jane Abrams from the collection in the General Library of the University of New Mexico of the original blocks used in publications of Willard "Spud" Johnson. From the 1920s until his death some forty years later, Johnson was both a participant and a perceptive observer of the literary and artistic scene of Santa Fe and Taos. The little magazine *Laughing Horse* is the most widely known of the publications with which Johnson was connected.

The illustrative blocks used by Johnson are significant enough in their own right to merit further investigation and study. For the most part, their identification and attribution are yet to be worked out. Two of the illustrations appearing in this book can be identified through their publication in *Laughing Horse*. The meditation opposite the preface was composed by Ward Lockwood. The tough old rooster opposite this page is from a drawing by Frieda Lawrence.

83

This book was
composed by the University of New Mexico Printing Plant
in Linotype Fairfield with hand-set Bulmer display,
printed by the University of New Mexico Printing Plant
on Warren's Olde Style paper, and
bound by The Becktold Company
in Holliston Kingston cloth.
Designed by Emmy Ezzell.